fə

JAUME SUBIRANA (Barcelona, 1963) is a writer, translator, and professor of Literature at the Universitat Pompeu Fabra. He has published seven collections of poetry, the latest being *La hac/The Silent Letter*. In 1988 he won Catalan poetry's most prestigious prize, the Carles Riba. In 2011, he was awarded the Gabriel Ferrater prize for *Una pedra sura*. He has published various essays, three volumes of award-winning diaries, and has translated Billy Collins, Seamus Heaney (with Pauline Ernest), Ted Kooser (with Miquel Àngel Llauger), Berta Piñán, Gary Snyder (with José Luis Regojo), R.S. Thomas and the children's poetry of Robert Louis Stevenson into Catalan. He is currently the vice-president of PEN Català. When he can, he enjoys listening to music, going fishing, daydreaming, and travelling.

CHRISTOPHER WHYTE (Glasgow, 1952) writes his own poetry in Scottish Gaelic, with his sixth collection *Ceum air Cheum/Step by Step* (2019) being nominated for two national awards. Between 1995 and 2000 he published four novels in English and he has translated into English the poetry of Rilke and Pasolini, as well as poets from Catalan, Croatian and Hungarian. Whyte is also known for his groundbreaking, innovative and at times controversial work researching and critiquing Scottish literature, with particular reference to literary theory, gender and queer studies. Whyte left a distinguished career as an academic in 2005 to devote himself entirely to writing. Currently he divides his time between Budapest and Prague.

THE SILENT LETTER

LETTER

JAUME SUBIRANA

TRANSLATED BY CHRISTOPHER WHYTE

FUM D'ESTAMPA PRESS LTD.
LONDON - BARCELONA

This translation has been published in Great Britain
by Fum d'Estampa Press Limited 2021

001

Cover quote by Manuel Castaño, *El Pais*

The moral right of the author and translator has been asserted
Set in Minion Pro

Printed and bound by TJ Books Limited, Padstow, Cornwall
A CIP catalogue record for this book is available from the British Library

ISBN: 978-1-9162939-9-1

Series design by 'el mestre' Rai Benach

This work was translated with the help of a grant from the Institut Ramon Llull.

LLLL institut
ramon llull
Catalan Language and Culture

fə

FUM D'ESTAMPA PRESS

CONTENTS

II

THE SILENT
LETTER

Man, sometimes it takes you a long time to sound like yourself.

MILES DAVIS

NADIR

Pintor del cel i les estrelles,
Van Gogh va escriure al seu germà:
"És meu, en certa forma,
el gira-sol".
Miro el cel i els meus versos:
els reconec i sempre
se m'escapen.
Vull dir que no tinc res,
em tenen, si de cas.
En certa forma jo sóc seu.
Dels gira-sols.

NADIR

Painter of sky and stars,
Van Gogh wrote to his brother:
"In a certain way the sunflower
is mine."
I look at the sky then at my poems:
I recognise them, yet
they constantly elude me.
What I mean is, I own nothing -
if anything, they own me.
In a certain way I'm theirs -
the sunflowers'.

I

A LA MANERA DE RUMI

No destensis l'arc encara,
diu la fletxa amb plomes blanques
al delit de disparar-la.

AFTER RUMI

Don't slacken the bow quite yet,
the white-feathered arrow tells
the delight of shooting it.

CARRER 84

Som a dins d'un núvol
de nit i de llums.
A baix al carrer
els cotxes naveguen,
al pis vint-i-u
el vent i la pluja
encenen els llamps
damunt del balcó
des d'on ens mirem
la pluja a les fosques,
la pluja escrivint-se
minúscula als vidres,
la pluja dient-nos
les hores futures:
quantes i per què,
anant cap a on,
quants carrers encara
abans d'arribar
al nostre destí.
Tot aquí apuntat
amb lletra esquitxada,
regalims i esclats,
i tot va esborrant-se.

84TH STREET

We're in a cloud
of night and lights.
Below cars navigate
along the street,
in Flat 21
the wind and the rain
light the lamps
above the balcony
from which we watch
the rain in the darkness,
the rain's tiny writing
on the windows,
the rain telling us
of future hours:
how many, why,
directed where,
how many more streets
before we meet
our destiny.
All noted here
in spattered writing,
trickles, flashes,
self-erasing.

CHIKUDO
(TINTA I PINTURA SOBRE SEDA)

Un cirerer florit. Dues branques d'un cirerer florit. Fulles i flors, marró i blanc, de dues branques d'un cirerer florit. Cada flor, una per una. Cada fulla. I totes alhora. Fa dos-cents anys al Japó. Ara i aquí. Cireres.

CHIKUDO
(INK AND PAINT ON SILK)

A flowering cherry tree. Two branches of a cherry tree. Leaves and flowers, dark brown and white, on two branches of a cherry tree. Each flower, taken singly. Each leaf. And then them all together. In Japan two hundred years ago. Here and now. Cherries.

ELS ARBRES I NOSALTRES

Tot ve a ser un joc d'escales.
Aquestes personetes ínfimes
al peu del sequoia són
de fet immenses al costat
de les llavors etèries i l'ocell.
Enormes i minúsculs, pedra i pols,
riu i la gota a punt de caure
mirant alegres a la càmera.
Tan alts, tan sols, tan vells,
els arbres i nosaltres.

THE TREES AND US

In the end it's all a matter of scale.
These tiny little people
at the foot of the sequoia
are in fact huge compared
to the ethereal seeds and the bird.
Immense and tiny, stone and dust,
the river and the drop about to fall
gaze cheerfully into the camera.
So tall, so old, so lonely –
the trees and us.

FIORD

Obert, ample, núvols, pla, pluja, sol, pluja, pedra, mar, verds, marrons, grisos, verds, riu, cascades, molsa, més cascades, herba, rierol, fils d'aigua, llac, guals, neu, glaç, horitzó, cobalt, ocells, ovelles, herba alta, cabanes, tanques, perspectiva. Enfora i endins i amunt en una sola paraula, si existís.

FJORD

Open, broad, clouds, flat, rain, sun, rain, stone, sea, greens, browns, greys, greens, river, waterfalls, moss, more waterfalls, grass, a streamlet, running water, a lake, crossing places, snow, ice, skyline, cobalt blue, birds, sheep, long grass, cabins, fences, view. Outside, inside, above in just one word, if that existed.

HAC

November always seemed to me
the Norway of the year.

EMILY DICKINSON, carta a Lavinia (1864)

La tarda sembla un vespre. Els ocells volen baix.
Un esquirol s'enfila dalt de tot de l'avet
com una taca viva per entre troncs pelats.

Al novembre el ponent remuga taciturn.
Un dia més del compte, canta Dylan de fons,
a tots dos ens sap greu. Qui sap si té raó.

L'esquirol torna i diu, parlant en noruec:
"Està a punt de passar. Ve la neu, la quietud",
i hi ha una pausa muda com la hac de l'hivern.

THE SILENT LETTER

*November always seemed to me
the Norway of the year.*

EMILY DICKINSON, letter to Lavinia (1864)

This afternoon could be an evening. Birds fly low.
A squirrel runs all the way up the fir tree,
living mark between bare trunks.

November. The west wind mutters, taciturn.
One more day gone, Dylan singing in the background.
We both regret it. Who knows if he's right?

Coming back, the squirrel speaks Norwegian:
"It's about to happen. Soon comes snow, and peace".
A silent pause next. Winter's silent letter.

HAVENT ESCAMPAT

La pluja calla
damunt del calendari.
Agost amb gotes.

THE RAIN STOPS

Raindrops dumb
above the calendar.
A dripping August.

HOTEL (STILL LIFE)

En tota la paret, tan gran,
només hi ha un quadre amb un rectangle
dins d'un altre rectangle.
Me'l miro i no el sé veure tot.
Vull dir que no s'entén què diu,
què es veu al quadre, mig suspès
cap a la dreta a l'altra banda
dels angles tristos del televisor.
Mentre m'hi acosto penso en les natures mortes,
en peixos, fruita, un bol, flors seques, l'oboè.
El telèfon no sona, no truquen a la porta.
Vaig entrant dins del quadre.

HOTEL (STILL LIFE)

It's such a big wall,
just one painting, a rectangle
inside another rectangle.
I look but cannot see it all.
Meaning, what it says cannot be understood,
what the painting shows, hanging halfway
to the right beyond
the television's mournful corners.
Going close, I think of still lifes,
fish, fruit, a bowl, dried flowers, an oboe.
The phone doesn't ring, no one knocks at the door.
I start entering the picture.

INDIAN SUMMER

One clover, and a bee,
And revery.

EMILY DICKINSON

Han tornat els ocells.
El cel duu roba clara
d'abans de la calor.
Escolto les abelles
resant a sota el ràfec,
vora les cambres buides,
mentre a les mans obertes
s'adorm la marinada.
Libem un sacrament
de llum i de silenci.

INDIAN SUMMER

One clover, and a bee,
And revery.

EMILY DICKINSON

The birds are back.
The sky wears white
for before heat.
I listen to the bees
praying beneath the eaves,
outside the empty rooms,
while in my open hands
the sea breeze falls asleep.
We sip a sacrament
of light and silence.

JONÀS A LA GARONA

ora chè notte
che la mia vita mi pare
una corolla
di tenebre

GIUSEPPE UNGARETTI, "I fiumi"

I

Mil nou-cents trenta-tres, a Provença, a l'estiu.
Al primer traspuntar d'una llum desbordada
Josep Carner, poeta, mirava el Pirineu
ombrejat a migdia, pensava en Barcelona,
pensava en Viladrau i aquells avellaners
que no veuria més a taules desparades
ara que faltaria el seu germà Guerau,
enamorat de núvols, de faigs i de muntanyes.
Camins, una tartana, les ombres i la llum,
llum a sobre de l'aigua amb ombres ondulades.
Li va semblar que veia un peix més gran al riu
movent-se sota el pont, i llavors el cridaven.
L'havia fet venir un amic dels amics
de la llengua amagada de Muret i Tolosa
i volia portar-lo a conèixer aquell sud
al nord de Catalunya i tan a prop d'Hendaia.

II

Van anar a Sant Bertran amb un cotxe llogat.

JONAH BY THE GARONNE

*ora chè notte
che la mia vita mi pare
una corolla
di tenebre*

GIUSEPPE UNGARETTI, "I fiumi"

I

Nineteen thirty-three, summer in Provence.
Light has just reached the point of brimming over
as the poet Josep Carner observes the Pyrenees
in shadow at midday, thinking of Barcelona,
thinking of Viladrau, those hazelnut trees
he would never see again, the tables cleared
now his brother Guerau is no more,
in love with clouds, beech trees and mountains.
Paths, a country cart, light and shadow,
light on the water's rippling waves.
He thinks he catches sight of a bigger fish in the river
moving under the bridge and then they call him.
Guest of a friend of friends
of the hidden tongue of Muret and Toulouse
who wanted to introduce him to that south
north of Catalonia, so close to Hendaye.

II

They went in a rented car to Sant Bertran

Van pujar pels carrers empedrats de la vila
a veure la gran sala del castell-catedral
i llavors, a la tarda, el van dur per la plana
travessant verdes prades on un dia hi hagué
la capital romana de tota la província,
a conèixer Sant Just ("Sé que us agradarà").
Era Sant Pau del Camp més alt i enmig dels camps,
navegant en la llum d'una tarda embaumada.
Sant Just i sant Pastor presidien la nau
–la sang dels innocents, les veus de criatura–
i l'amic li parlava dels temps de Barcelona.
Massa coses alhora, massa a prop tot de casa
havent de viure'n lluny. Va seure a descansar:
l'any vinent, al febrer, en faria cinquanta.
Al fons, en la tenebra, amunt de l'alta nau,
es veia un marbre clar dessota una finestra:
era una estela llarga amb un rectangle buit
entre dues escenes amb bèsties i persones.
S'hi va acostar en silenci. Va demanar més llum.

III

Al plafó de l'esquerra des de dalt d'una barca
un home en llança un altre a la boca d'un peix
de grans dents esmolades amb mig cos fora l'aigua.
Al plafó de la dreta l'home surt mig reptant
de la boca del peix i s'ajeu més enllà
alliberat i nu, a l'empar d'unes fulles.
Entremig no hi ha res, un tros de pedra buida
al centre del retaule, com si hi faltés el Crist.

and climbed the stony village streets
to see the great hall of the castle-cathedral.
Then, in the afternoon, they took him across the plain,
through verdant meadows where one day there lay
the Roman capital of the entire province,
to visit Sant Just ("I know you'll like it").
Higher than Sant Pau, surrounded by fields,
afloat in the light of a balmy afternoon.
Echoes of the Barcelona church,
Sant Just and Sant Pastor, in the nave
– blood of the innocents, children's voices –
and his friend spoke of the times in Barcelona.
Too much all at once, too close to the home
he had to live far from. He sat down to rest:
next year, in February, he'd be fifty.
In the background darkness, above the high nave,
a gleam of marble under a window:
a broad bas-relief with an empty rectangle
between two scenes of animals and people.
Approaching in silence, he asked for more light.

III

On the left-hand panel, a man is throwing
another from a boat into a fish's mouth,
its teeth big and sharp, half out of the water.
On the right-hand panel, the man emerges
half crawling from the mouth, then lies to one side
free and naked, protected by some leaves.
Nothing in the middle, empty stone
in the centre of the reredos, as if Christ should be there.

IV

Ha escrit, ha viatjat, ha conegut, recorda,
manté una família, és cònsol, viuen bé.
De vegades li sembla que navega escapant-se
com un príncep inútil, com desvagat hereu.
Es mira el carreu net clavat a la paret.
Podria ser romà, gòtic o noucentista.
Hi veu Jonàs, és clar, quan el llancen al mar,
i Jonàs sent deixat pel gran peix a la platja
a la vora de Jaffa a sota un emparrat.
No sap que les onades, Jonàs i la balena
i tres anys, no tres dies, l'esperen aviat
amb la mort de son pare, la de Carmen al Líban
i la guerra i l'exili i tants camins incerts.
Ell no sap què l'espera però mira l'estela
i mira el morter vell i brut de la paret
prop dels perfils perfectes dels homes, de les plantes,
del mar i del gran peix, es mira el quadre en blanc
entre una escena i l'altra i recita dos versos
Tu que rebats amb fúria la porta de l'estiu
i que la clau en llences al doll inflat del riu.
"Hauríem de marxar", li diuen des de fora.

V

Enlluernats pel sol, l'amic que el convidava
parla d'anar a Tolosa, de llibres, de projectes,
de França i de Provença, d'Espanya i Catalunya,
de llengües, de poemes, d'amics, de la República...
Al cotxe de tornada segueixen la Garona
i l'amic parla i parla i travessen el riu

IV

He has written, travelled, seen, remembered,
supports a family, is consul, they live well.
Sometimes he feels his voyage is the flight
of a useless prince, an heir with nothing to do.
He observes the neat rectangle attached to the wall.
It could be Roman, Gothic, early 20th century.
Obviously it shows Jonah being tossed into the sea,
then the big fish leaving him on the beach
by Jaffa beneath a vineyard.
Not knowing that the waves, Jonah and the whale,
three years and not three days await him,
his father's death, Carmen's in Lebanon,
the war, exile, so many uncertain paths.
Not knowing what lies ahead, he nonetheless observes
the bas-relief, that stark, ageing panel on the wall
next to the perfect outlines of men and plants,
of the sea and the big fish, observes the blank space
between one scene and the other, pronounces two lines:
"You who furiously slam summer's door shut
and toss its key into the river's swollen torrent."
From outside comes "It's time for us to go".

V

The sunlight dazes them. The friend who invited him
talks of going to Toulouse, of books and projects,
of France and Provence, of Spain and Catalonia,
languages, poems, friends, of the Republic...
Driving back they follow the Garonne,
his friend talks incessantly, they cross and recross

unes quantes vegades. "És aigua catalana",
sent que l'altre li diu, "no som tan lluny de casa".
Quants anys fa que marxà? Quants mars i quantes cases?
Com l'aigua, ha anat passant, estrany en terra estranya,
com les pedres i el marbre. Per un moment la imatge
del gran peix apareix en un revolt del riu
mentre sent el soroll de la terra esclafada,
i diria haver vist reflectits sota els arbres
el profeta i els nens en una aigua enrogida
pel ponent o el destí, les cares dels dos màrtirs
i Jonàs i l'amic submergint-se en l'obaga
entre un mar de cigales. El sol es nega al riu.
A dalt de la muntanya un núvol, un sol núvol,
perdut o rescatat, aombra la Garona.
Potser en faci un poema, amb el peix i les fulles
i sant Just i l'estela finament treballada,
amb el quadrat en blanc i l'aigua enterbolida
i el silenci de Déu en la nau a les fosques.
Ha vingut per tres dies. L'estiu toca a la fi.

the river several times. "Catalan water",
he hears the other say, "we're not far from home".
How long since he left? How many seas and homes?
Like the water, on its way, a stranger in strange lands,
like the stones and the marble. For a moment he sees
the big fish's image in a bend of the river,
hears the sound of trampled earth, could say
he had seen the prophet, the children reflected
under the trees, in water reddened by
fate or the west wind, the two martyrs' faces,
and Jonah and his friend sinking into the darkness
of a sea of cicadas. The sun drowns in the river.
Above the mountain, a cloud, one single cloud,
lost or redeemed, casts its shadow on the Garonne.
Maybe he can make a poem of it - the fish, the leaves,
Saint Just and the delicate sculpted relief,
the blank rectangle and the troubled water
and God silent in the darkness of the nave.
He's here for three days. Summer is at an end.

MALPAÍS

Pedra esberlada, seca.
Pedra marró, vermella, negra.
Pedra a la vora i lluny
caiguda a plom, estesa,
amuntegada, oferta.
Pedra a la mà d'un déu de pedra
i l'ànima de déu potser
colgada sota la pedrera.

BAD PLACE

Dry, chipped stone.
Brown, red, green stone.
Stone near and far,
plummeting, stretching,
piled up, offered.
Stone in the hand of a stone god
and maybe, buried underneath
the quarry, god's soul.

BUSON A VENÈCIA

La resplendor daurada
del sol damunt les pedres
cansades de ser belles.

BUSON IN VENICE

The gilded splendour of
the sun on stones
tired of being beautiful.

MEMENTO VIVERE

We asked for signs, the signs were sent.

LEONARD COHEN

"Un moment, ara torno". I s'allunya
havent deixat com un senyal, penjant,
la bossa a la cadira espellifada.
La calma, la bellesa, l'alegria
són temporals, i tot llavors en parla.
O bé la bossa és una bossa sola
com tu llegint les restes del cafè,
cada sopar és sempre aquest sopar,
aquella absència, el goig evaporat.
Pel vi, pel vidre, pels canals
passa un cometa.

MEMENTO VIVERE

We asked for signs, the signs were sent.

"Back in a moment". And off she goes
leaving her bag dangling
like a signal on the battered chair.
Calm, beauty, joy are lodged
in time, everything speaks of them.
Or perhaps the bag is merely that,
like you reading the coffee grounds,
every dinner will always be this dinner,
that absence, joy gone up in smoke.
In the wine, in the glass, along the canals
a comet's passage.

PONTE STORTO

El reflex de l'aigua
a la pedra clara
de sota del pont.
En diuen migdia.
Un altre en diria
la llum de la son.

PONTE STORTO

Water reflected
on the bright stone
beneath the bridge.
Midday, they say.
Another might say
drowsy light.

FONDAMENTA

Xiulen trens en la nit
escapant-se de l'illa:
duen llums molt petits
cap a terra i fan veus
amb la via i les llanxes
a intervals regulars.
A la nit penso en trens
carregats a l'andana
esperant que m'adormi
per anar-se'n d'aquí,
fondamenta dels somnis,
llumenets del sentit.
Els que tornen van buits,
llarga corda a les fosques
sotragant en silenci,
sotragant cap a mi.

FONDAMENTA

Escaping from the island
trains whistle through the night:
carrying to the mainland
tiny lights, on the causeway
their voices alternating
at regular intervals
with the water taxis.
At night I think of trains
full up at the platform
waiting to depart
until I fall asleep,
dreamladen *fondamenta*,
little lights of meaning.
When they return they're empty,
a long rope in the darkness
clattering in the silence,
clattering towards me.

NEU (SAY GOODBYE)

El pneumàtic de la nit alenteix a la cruïlla, enfredorit.

Les hores petites respiren cada vegada més fluix, quallen a poc a poc en aquest silenci mineral dels arbres, es tornen neu incògnita, com un present lliurat i abandonat en ofrena als plecs de la matinada.

La neu, tanta. Dóna'n les gràcies. Hauràs tingut l'honor que passi amb tu la nit en vetlla i, quan obris els ulls, demà, mesos després, fins el record se n'haurà fos.

Ara, avui, tens tot al voltant un llençol blanc gebrat.

SNOW (SAY GOODBYE)

Catching cold, night's tyre slows down at the crossroads.

The breathing of the small hours gradually weakens, they congeal progressively in this mineral silence of the trees, assuming the disguise of snow, like a present delivered, left in offering to the folds of dawn.

So much snow. Give thanks. You'll have had the privilege of spending a wakeful night with it, and when your eyes open, to-morrow, months later, even the memory of it will have melted.

Now, today, all around you, a white sheet covered in frost.

SAN ANTOLÍN DE BEÓN
(VERSIÓ LLIURE DE BERTA PIÑÁN)

Quin material estrany i absurd ets, poesia:
desveles amb detall les tenebres de l'ànima
i no arribes a dir el color en què es congria
la pàtina del mar als seus ulls a la tarda.

SAN ANTOLÍN DE BEÓN
(FREE VERSION AFTER BERTA PIÑÁN)

What strange, absurd matter you are, poetry:
revealing in detail the darkness of the soul
unable to tell the colour of the sea's patina
growing solid in her eyes when afternoon comes.

TARJA D'EMBARCAMENT

La mica de vi que deixes al vas.
L'amiga d'ahir a l'ombra d'un braç.
L'estona al matí pensant en la mare.
El Brodsky llegit que no saps on para.
Un tros de camí on vas tenir por.
El fil sense fi de no dir que no.
La veu de dir sí. Les claus de les cases.
Aquell bisturí. La funda de gasa.
Tot es queda aquí, i tu te n'en vas.

BOARDING PASS

A little wine stain in the glass.
Yesterday's friend on a shadowy arm.
Thinking of your mother in the morning.
Brodsky's book you cannot lay your hands on.
A stretch of road on which you felt afraid.
The endless thread of never saying no.
Yes finding a voice. Keys to your homes.
That lancet. Sheathed in gauze.
All staying here, while you depart.

TŶ NEWYDD

La tarda em plou al cap
un aire dolç i fred
que borda rere els núvols.
Em miro els bens pintats
al llom d'aquest paisatge
i sóc el verd del prat
a dins de cada gota,
ballant a les vocals.

TŶ NEWYDD

Afternoon rains on my head
a sweet, chill air
that barks behind the clouds.
I look at the sheep painted
at the back of the landscape
and am the meadow's green
inside every drop,
dancing on the vowels.

UN POEMA PER A KATHE

A Berlín vam esmorzar a la Literaturhaus per anar després
a veure el museu de Kathe Kolwitz, allà al costat. Hi anava
per recomanació del Narcís, amb el seu poema al cap i amb
la vaga idea d'escriure llavors alguna cosa que hi dialogués.
Feia molta calor. L'obra de Kolwitz és corprenedora. La seva
biografia impressiona. El carbonet esborrona, quin traç trist,
fosc tan de veritat. I el que me n'ha quedat gravat és el groc i
el negre brunzent de les abelles mentre esmorzàvem, la por de
la Maria a les abelles a la llum esclatant del sol d'agost, els ulls
i la mà de la Maria, que pinta com un àngel i mira d'espantar
una i una altra les abelles, cada abella, tantes abelles.

A POEM FOR KATHE

In Berlin we had breakfast at the Literaturhaus then went to
see the Kathe Kollwitz museum next door. Narcís had told
me to go, with his poem in my head and the vague idea of
writing something that dialogued with it. It was very hot.
Kollwitz's work overwhelms. A life story beyond belief. Horri-
fying charcoal, such sad strokes, so much dark truth. Etched
in my mind afterwards, the buzzing yellow and black of the
bees at breakfast, Maria afraid of them as the August sunlight
exploded, her eyes, her hand that paints like an angel, doing
its best to scare them off one by one, each bee, so many bees.

II

AIXÍ

El temps d'aclucar els ulls,
de dibuixar una lletra,
d'escurar el vas amb set,
de llepar-li l'esquena,
d'escoltar una cançó.
Així, tota una vida.

LIKE THAT

Long enough to close your eyes,
sketch a letter,
gulp the glass down,
lick her shoulder,
listen to a song.
A whole life, like that.

CINE FAMILIAR

Les veus, les veus.
El pis és la pantalla.
I mentre seus
esclata una crispeta
tendra, la neu
dels riures reverbera.
Tan lleu, tot teu.
Tan lleu i teu.

FAMILY CINEMA

You see the voices.
Our flat's the screen.
As you sit there,
a popcorn explodes,
like snow, laughter
reverberates.
So light, all yours.
So light, and yours.

CUSTODIS

"Això és meu", i sento
la bocassa pudent
de la falsa promesa.
Tenir, no tenim res:
si de cas som custodis
dels ulls que ens han mirat,
dels noms dels fills i els pares,
de les quatre paraules
amb què parem la taula,
de la pols i la cendra,
de la tela, del marbre,
del lòbul de l'orella,
de l'arbre i la muntanya,
de la por d'una nit,
del paper, de Venècia,
de la fusta, del foc,
de les ales de l'àngel
invisible i esquerp
sorneguer rere nostre
mentre fem i desfem
i refem les promeses.

GUARDIANS

"That's mine" – the nasty,
putrid taste
of a false promise.
Nothing is mine or ours:
if anything we get on trust
eyes that observed us,
our children's names, our parents',
the few words
with which we lay the table,
for dust, for ash,
for cloth, marble
and earlobe,
for tree and mountain,
for one night's fear,
for paper, Venice,
wood, fire,
for the invisible, impalpable
wings of the angel
who scoffs at our backs
as we make, unmake,
remake promises.

DEL NATURAL

Una paret
plena de claus.
L'ombra que fa
tot el que hi falta.

SKETCH

A wall
full of nails.
The shadow of every-
thing missing.

DEMÀ

Any nou, dia d'estrena,
pàgina neta al tac
de mesos apinyats
com una bossa plena,
com un llençol en blanc,
llarguíssim esmorzar.
Ho sé: només comença
allò ja començat.
Escric la lletra a.
Surto a comprar una llesca
pel ganivet del pa.
Quan torno, som demà.

TOMORROW

New Year, for trying on
new things, a spotless page
crammed with months
like a full bag,
like a white bedsheet,
a never-ending breakfast.
I know: only what's already
begun can begin.
I write the letter "a".
Go out to buy a slice
of bread the knife can cut.
I come back, it's tomorrow.

DESEMBRE

Llenço l'agenda.
Mentrestant, al carrer,
volen les fulles.

DECEMBER

I toss away the diary.
While, in the street,
leaves fly like pages.

DUSK

Llegim i som llegits
amb una ala de llum
a dins de cada pàgina.
Ocells que no veiem,
marees, abraçades,
perfils de les paraules
a l'alba de paper,
corrent de tinta blava
al fil de l'horitzó.
Les lletres són nosaltres,
surant al panorama.

DUSK

We read and we are read
with a wing of light
inside every page.
Birds that we don't see,
tides, the hugs we gave,
the silhouettes of words
on a paper dawn,
blue ink running along
the edge of the skyline.
We ourselves the letters
floating in the background.

ESPECTACLE

Els arbres ballen i tremolen
a dins del vidre,
com si la llum els excités,
el vent els estirés,
la perspectiva els fes
ull i budell, tot tu
ballant i tremolant
a l'escenari.
Matí d'abril
tot tu,
ballant al vidre.

SHOW

The trees dance and tremble
in the window pane
as if excited by the light,
as if stretched by the wind,
as if perspective made them
eye and bowel, all
of you dancing and trembling
up on stage.
An April morning,
all of it
you dancing in the pane.

HABITACIÓ 427

Maduixa liquada,
ungla de sol, de síndria,
senyal, robí, magrana,
esquitx de rosa viva,
corona que s'esguerra,
un tret de llum als peus,
el so que no sonava.
Aquella gota a terra.

ROOM 427

Liquid strawberry,
sun, watermelon fingernail,
a mark, a ruby, a pomegranate,
a living, rose-coloured splash,
a mutilated crown,
bullet hole of light at our feet,
a sound that made no sound.
That drop there on the floor.

LA BRANCA

Voldria ser la branca de la nit
on el sentit s'adorm i tot respira
acompassat, amb tiges, amb un niu
petit on s'arrecera la mirada
quan gairebé ja no s'hi veu
i déu despara la jornada.
Ser branca de la nit
i res més, ara.

THE BRANCH

I'd like to be the night-time branch
where meaning sleeps, where everything
can breathe in peace, with stems, a small
nest in which the gaze takes refuge
when the eye can barely see, and
god clears the day's dishes away.
A night time branch
now, nothing more.

LLEGINT ANDRADE

Obre les cuixes:
llum i la pell.

Un solc és l'aire
sobre la forma

tant com la terra
dels cavallons.

READING ANDRADE

Parting thighs:
light, the skin.

The air a furrow
on that shape

the same way land
rises in ridges.

MAGNIFICAT

Seure a escriure un Magníficat
i deixar el full en blanc.
Voler ser com Vivaldi,
voler sonar com Bach,
i enfilar versos grisos
dels que no saps on van
amb la paraula "meva",
el verb "magnificar"
i aquell terrible "Dominum"
sonant com un metall
enterrat a la gola,
com restes del naufragi
dels jos en alta mar.
Tenir-ho ben après,
haver estudiat els quadres,
les notes, les paraules
i no saber dir res.

MAGNIFICAT

Sitting down to write a "Magnificat"
and leaving the page untouched.
Wanting to be Vivaldi,
wanting to play like Bach,
linking dull verses together
not knowing where they're going
in them the word "mine",
the verb "magnify",
that terrible "Dominum"
sounding like metal
deep within the throat,
like remains of the shipwreck
of "I"s far out at sea.
Knowing it by heart,
having studied the staves,
the notes and words
and able to say nothing.

MOLÈSTIA

quants anys passats als bars
a les cafeteries
mirant de fer que no
ballés la taula
plegant paper
buscant trossets
de fusta procurant
no recolzar-te fer
que no es mogués el marbre
anant a un altre lloc
com si el ball
mínim del sobre fos dolent
sense adonar-te que la gràcia
precisament
és que les coses ballin
que només una fusta
està sempre tranquil·la
la de la caixa envernissada
allà ben encaixada
a l'infinit

BOTHERSOME

so many years at bars
in cafés
trying to stop the table
shaking
folding paper
looking for bits
of wood trying not
to lean on them so
the marble won't move
going somewhere else
as if the slightest
movement of the top were bad
without realising that precisely
what matters is
things start shaking
only a piece of wood
can always be at peace
as with the varnished box
deposited securely
within eternity

ON MIRO LA BET ANAR-SE'N TOTA SOLA CAP A COL·LEGI

se'n va de cara al dia
fa com que arriba tard
em diu adéu a penes
alçant molt poc la mà
somriu quan repeteixo
compte passa-t'ho bé
suposo que somreia
tranquil·la tiba el fil
de nou anys fins al dia
amb ella dreta aquí
veient a la motxilla
la dansa dels clauers
paraules despintades
un nom fent-se petit
el cap els peus les cames
que vas tenir a les mans
saltant a la vorera
per on els fills se'n van

WHERE I WATCH BETH DEPARTING
ALL ON HER OWN TO SCHOOL

off to her day she goes
as if she were late
with not quite a goodbye
barely lifting her hand
she smiles when I repeat
take care, have a good time
I suppose she smiled the same
calm, tense smile all the way
through nine years till the day
when she stands right here
watching how the keys
dance on her bag
words fading out
a shrinking name
head feet and legs
my hands would hold
jumping along the pavement
that leads children away

PROCESSIONAL

Veure passar l'estona
com veus passar la gent:
pensar noms i penyores
i oblidar el pensament.
Veure com tot s'estira
i estirar-ne els colors.
Pensar que som a fira,
badar, no tenir por.
Afegir-te a la fila
serè, no dir que no.

IN PROCESSION

To watch the moment pass
as you watch people pass:
to think of names and pledges
and then forget the thought.
To watch it all stretch out
and stretch the colours further.
To think we're at a fair:
stand gaping, feel no fear.
To take your place in the
calm parade, not say no.

S'ACOSTA EL DIA

¿No sents com calla tot,
com s'apaivaga l'obsessió,
com s'esclarissa l'ombra,
com desaprens camins?
S'acosta el dia.
Ho saps però no hi penses
o fas com que no hi penses
per si no tens raó.
I tanmateix s'acosta el dia
que et vas dir que prendries
alguna decisió.
Ara mateix la por que sents
et sembla que no és
la d'un final sinó
la del punt i seguit,
com un que fa l'escala
i no diu do.
S'acosta el dia
per a la covardia,
per a la gallardia,
pel sí, pel no.

DAY APPROACHES

Can't you hear how everything falls silent,
obsessions are appeased,
how the shadows disperse,
how you unlearn paths?
Day approaches.
You know, give it no thought
or act as if you didn't
just in case you are wrong.
The day approaches nonetheless
on which you told yourself
you'd take a certain decision.
You think right now what makes
you afraid is not an ending
but rather breaking off,
as someone sings a scale
but never reaches "doh".
Day approaches
a day for cowardice,
a day for bravery,
a day for yes, for no.

SETANTA VEGADES SET

¿D'aquells set dies quin
badava més del compte,
o quin dels set pecats
encara no he comès?
¿Quin dels set nans dirà
que em va veure a la mina
posant-me a la butxaca
el diamant d'un altre?
Cada matí prometo
comptar fins a setanta,
i compto i em descompto
trastocat per la set.

SEVENTY TIMES SEVEN

Which of those seven days
saw me less attentive,
which of the seven sins
have I yet to commit?
Which of the seven dwarfs will say
he saw me in the mine
putting in my pocket
someone else's diamond?
Every morning I promise
to count to seventy,
I count and then lose count,
driven crazy by thirst.

TOCAR UN ESCRIPTOR MORT

A Màrius Sampere

Tocar un escriptor mort és desenterrar paraules,
és triar palets de riu per llançar-los a la lluna
i seure a esperar la veu amb un fil blanc a les mans.

Tocar un escriptor mort és girar-li les costures
com ens va ensenyar la mare i mirar-nos les mans buides,
és furgar-nos les butxaques mentre cauen les monedes.

Tocar un escriptor mort abans de la seva mort
és el que sol fer la gent: donar les gràcies, somriure,
quedar per veure'ns aviat, agafar-lo fort pel braç.

Jo vull tocar-lo ja mort, després que se n'hagi anat,
buscar la vella energia que la nit ha refredat:
palpar-li les alegries i cada llibre i el cap

fins a la llengua apagada, jugar amb l'anell de l'escriba
entre els dits amb què desfeia les idees i la rima,
burxar la punta dels dits al final de les mans fortes.

Tocar la mort amb paraules, no tocar paraules mortes.
Agafar la pedra plana i posar-me-la a la boca
com si fos un tros de riu, i fluir i omplir-la tota.

TOUCHING A DEAD WRITER

for Màrius Sampere

Touching a dead writer means digging up words,
means picking river pebbles to throw them at the moon,
sitting waiting for a voice, a white thread in your hands.

Touching a dead writer means turning out his seams
the way our mother showed us, finding our hands empty,
means ransacking our pockets as the coins tumble out.

Touching a dead writer before he's dead
is what people usually do: thank him, and smile,
agree to meet up soon, take hold of his arm.

I want to touch him already dead, after he's gone,
to look for the old energy which night has chilled:
to touch what gave him joy, every book, his head

right to his silent tongue, to play with the writer's
ring amidst those fingers that undid ideas, rhymes,
to jab the finger tips at the end of those strong hands.

To touch death with words, not to touch dead words.
To take the flat stone and put it in my mouth
as if it were part of a river, to flow, filling it all.

TOMBES ROMANES

Tinc un quart d'hora lliure
al davant de la via sepulcral.
La meva agenda, aquesta calma;
el meu quart d'hora, aquests mil·lennis.
La plaça bull d'una altra dansa.

Buit i silenci,
clova per dins.
Tota la vida,
quinze minuts.
Som llengües mortes:
plens i perduts.

ROMAN TOMBS

A free quarter of an hour
before the road of tombs.
My diary, and this calm;
my fifteen minutes, these millennia.
On the square another dance seethes.

Emptiness and silence,
inside of a nut's shell.
An entire life,
fifteen minutes.
We are dead tongues:
fulfilled and lost.

TOT EL QUE ÉS SÒLID

Llevar-te de matí
al peu d'aquella esquena.
L'aroma del cafè
burlant la cullereta.
El raig d'aigua, la llum
esclatada a la dutxa.
El blanc on gravaràs
les ratlles d'una excusa.
Les molletes de pa
dormint a dins l'esquerda.
La gota d'oli clar
on el reflex s'esberla.
La clau a dins del pany,
la seva parla fina
com el tros de carrer
quan el sol hi patina.
El llum verd, el vermell
de la seva sabata.
Les llepades de pi
a dalt de la muntanya
i l'encàrrec antic
invocat no fa gaire.
Tot el que és sòlid, tot,
ve que es dissol en l'aire.

ALL THAT'S SOLID

Getting up in the morning
where that spine ends.
The fragrance of coffee
making fun of the teaspoon.
Water spouting, rainbows
of light in the shower.
The white in which you'll sculpt
the lines of an excuse.
Little crumbs of bread
asleep inside the crack.
The drop of clear oil
in which the light breaks up.
The key inside the lock,
its delicate speech
like the stretch of road
the sun casts its light on.
The green of a light,
the red of a shoe.
Pine tree strokes
on top of the mountain,
a long ago task
evoked just now.
All that's solid, I see
melting in the air.

TRES LLETRES (ALBADA)

Un teu dit al meu llavi,
la palma de la mà
perdent temps a l'esquena,
la pena, aquesta pena
en què la nit alena
volent que no s'acabin
les lletres de demà.

El meu llavi diu dit
i la mà va fent via
palpant impenitent
la riba del present:
som això, som moment.
Només respiraria,
tres lletres, una nit.

FIVE LETTERS (AUBADE)

Your finger on my lips,
the palm of your hand
wasting time on my back,
the pain, this pain with which
the night exhales itself
not wanting tomorrow's
letters to reach an end.

My lips say "index"
the hand goes its way
explores impenitent
the river bank of now:
we're this, we are a moment.
All I want to breathe
five letters and one night.

ACKNOWLEDGEMENTS

In *The Practice of the Wild*, Gary Snyder quotes an old Buddhist prayer which begins by evoking the three treasures we all should venerate: our masters, nature and our friends. I think this book contains plenty of each. In any case, to name a few names, "The Silent Letter" was written in Hartford, Connecticut, in the rear porch of the house Tom Harrington allowed to be mine for several months. "Buson in Venice" and the short Venice sequence which follows I owe to Enric Bou, master and friend. "San Antolín de Beón" is a tribute to Berta Piñán's poetry and to her knowing smile. "Tŷ Newydd" was written in Wales, in the writers' residence which bears this name, where I was invited by Sioned Puw Rowlands. "A Poem for Kathe" is dedicated to Narcís Comadira. And to Maria, obviously. "To Touch a Dead Writer" was the homage I chose to write on learning of the death of Màrius Sampere, who I led by the arm as he led me in poetry. Besides which I also want to record here my gratitude, for different reasons, to Sara Antoniazzi, Jordi Cornudella, Xènia Dyakonova, Miquel Àngel Llauger, Esteve Miralles, Simona Škrabec and Jordi Virallonga. As well as to Douglas Suttle and

Christopher Whyte, for making this English version possible.

TRANSLATOR'S NOTES

THE SILENT LETTER

The initial letter of the Catalan word for winter, 'hivern', is silent.

SEVENTY TIMES SEVEN

In Catalan, the word 'set' means both 'seven' and 'thirst'. In the first case it is masculine gender, in the second feminine. The pun cannot be reproduced in English.

FIVE LETTERS (AUBADE)

The title refers to the five letters of "night" and "index", as the Catalan title does to the three letters of "nit" and "dit".

VITA NOVA
BY JORDI GALVES

Georges Brassens, the last great French poet I am aware of, wrote about experiences as strange as they were classic, as disturbing as they were far from the ambient narcissism promoted by the majority of subjective essays, turned savage by rock & roll. Of Jaume Subirana's poetry I have the same certainty and consolation as when I read the Frenchman's; he speaks to me of myself while apparently writing about himself, proving a fine use of my limited time as I reread their verses, discreetly scattered like breadcrumb trails. I know he will be attentive, subtle, at times difficult to understand, never strident, but rather like one of those mayordoms from another time, holed up in a Scottish castle from another age, passing me a copy of *The Times*, open at the page he knows I want, the one with the crosswords and other ingenious exercises. Moderate exercises, living at the edge. A poet or writer is not great just because they have written one or two extraordinary pages or some loud, celebrated text, but rather because they stay focussed and awake, make few errors, and bore little. Or at least not regularly. The greatness of Oscar Wilde, to use a notorious example, is thanks to this and not of his scandalous use of Champagne bottles, regularly shooting them off with the precision and racket of Wellington's very own artillery. The greatness of Uncle Oscar is that he is always right, and you can trust in the fact that it will always be worth revisiting that which he has written for you. It seems the ant and the cicada have learnt to collaborate, singing their different songs in unison. Indeed, contemporary European poetry has gone from an oh! to an oh no, from expressive exhibitionism to verbal nutrition, from a gaseous state to liquid, from blind temerity to elemental prudence, from spitting at one's audience to hoping to make friends. Or acquaintances. I don't think I'm wrong when I say that Subirana's poetry dares to search out common sense and meaning in the midst of the experience, in the intimate biography steadily shedding itself of all unnecessary things until blossoming into an unexpected collection of visual, revolutionary Joan Brossa-esque poems. Visual because they cry out to be interpreted beyond the immediate obvious. A poetry as experimental as any other, as doubting as any other, but that sketches out a specific drawing, a slice of meaning, provisional comprehension, a harvest from within the fog.

Nicador Parra wrote that until his appearance poetry had been "the solemn idiot's paradise" for half a century. That the right to stupidity had finished, hopefully forever, hopefully for everyone. That poetry as a mental or verbal refuge – a place to redefine one's life – found itself ever more suffocated, and all in vain: its fingernails scraping insistently against the door every night. That life itself will always end by reclaiming its rights. It is most possible that from this conviction comes the reason Jaume Subirana writes like he does, as a discreet survivor of a determined continuity or tradition, a wiseman camouflaging himself well against his surroundings so as to stay alive, predator and child of predators, a poet fisherman and collector, opportunist and wanderer, inevitably another Robinson in the big city, another blue-collar worker wandering the countryside, an unexpected apprentice of Melville in today's extraordinary, fish-filled Mediterranean Sea. Or perhaps Stevenson's *Garden of Child's Verses*, translated by him into Catalan. He is both a poet as wild, pure and intellectual as Seamus Heaney (who he has also translated into Catalan) and T.S. Eliot: brave when we see him lost to the wilderness, twinned with the most insignificant reader of his verses, anxious and unsatisfied. Speechless, paradoxical and speculative like Philip, the ugliest of all the Larkins, overwhelmed by the human pulsations of sex and violence, by the plague that Doctor Freud unleashed on us from crowded Vienna. By means of a footnote, the dramatics of a number of genuine characters to appear throughout European poetry for the last hundred years, from W. B. Yeats up to present day, can be added to Jaume Subirana's personal biography.

In this book, culture is understood as – amongst many others – a way of life lived in private, though by no means a place to hide away from life, to run away from yourself. In that perhaps we can agree. And it's precisely because of this that the key to Jaume Subirana's biography, driven by poetry, allows us to experience this latest volume of work – *The Silent Letter* – when the poet is reaching his sixties. Firstly, as a simple testimony to his new autumnal style of life. A new start, a new life. But it is mostly as an exercise of coherence, the continuation of life, of writing, of his first book, published in 1985: *Pel viure extrem*. Yeats, ever the good father, was quoted, evoked, invoked as one might invoke a kindly forest spirit who, in a somehow predictable manner, announced with comforting sureness the sensation of protection under one of the greatest benevolent shadows in the game:

Bodily decrepitude is wisdom; young
We loved each other and were ignorant.

To realise that the quote you used thirty-five years ago when first presenting yourself as a poet doesn't seem, after so much time, to be foolish in its entirety – whether you want it or not, you've become another person – might confirm that your references aren't totally erroneous, that they as activities speak quite well of the Subirana personality as a trustworthy poet, constant and durable. A voice bringing us the language of Ausiàs March, of Jacint Verdaguer, of Mercè Rodoreda, of Gabriel Ferrater. A writer to have always trusted in untrustworthy writers and, like all professors, wary of wise, venerable books that claim to know the holy truth and so are full of magic, arcane solutions. He is a writer who recognises himself in scepticism, who agitates and protests with the possibility of infallible or, at least, moral certainty. It's through political propaganda that certain civil behaviour ends up being popularised, though ever limited at the moment of truth, to a few approximate recommendations, to a handful of rules, some preventions, insecurities, to certain oily taboos. There's no remedy: the solidity of contemporary man, one of the vanities of the world, is fatally expressed at its point of dissolving into fresh air (see one of the last poems) like a word on the wind, and our arrogance will ever be punished as imprudent, clumsy folly.

From here comes 2007's *Rapala* – probably his first masterpiece – in which Subirana lifts up his hands in celebration of intimate human satisfaction, primordial sensations, not only because they belong to life itself, but because they are the sole constituents that can be used to narrate any half-dignified bio-graphy of Subirana, as disconnected as possible from the blind gregariousness of mere sheep. Behind the colours, the aromas and particularly the irrepressible experience of tact that fill so many of Subirana's poems, we can see an obvious vindication of the senses that increase the act of living. We are not sure if they number five or more, but what is clear is that they contrast with the limitation and frustration, and the instable, traitorous, often terrified mind, overtaken by a daily life ever more astonished by the deafness of life towards human longing, as stubborn as an ox. Subirana's biography advances not so much as a predictable collection of apprenticeships, but through real learning, that of the main map made up of straight and curving, untrodden paths. Poverty is our ever faithful friend, our finest councillor, a universal experience drawing our gazes towards the horizon and the sky so as to predict the changes in the weather, to start every morning hoping for victory. The shipwreck is our greatest teacher, advising us to retire voluntarily from any lengthening of life before it's too late, to definitively unlearn the certainty of death. In the intensity of ignorance, the oblivion of the moment, we feel eternal and pure, a little like animals not knowing they are to die.

The Silent Letter is a bright, engaging book that somehow represents the survival of Subirana's original viure extrem but arriving along other, totally unexpected, contemporary routes, along other medias, other forms of expression and daring, playful arguments, of new perspectives or arguments from a Subirana still producing book after book with an unending enthusiasm, as any deeply vital, creative, continuing poet should. It is the radiant light of autumn, darting unexpectedly into one's eyes like that which was once described by Josep Carner via the landscapes of Mosa (and of Provence as is evoked here by the long poem that suggests a possible point of conception for *Nabí*, one of the great European works of poetry of the 20th century), where the margins are and always will be blankets of red and gold. It is the intentional, natural continuation of life that leads to the intentional, natural continuation of the celebration of scripture, only there where Josep Carner, poet of infinite Catalan odes, left it do we pick up the thread once again, sending reflections of an Horatian life everywhere, making it possible to forget about thought. It is in the shared intimacy of the autumnal biography in which Jaume Subirana, curtailed and apprehensive, inevitably reflects and embraces Carner with the same certainty that great-grandchildren keep their cherished great-grandparents alive. We are presented with a curious, nosey Subirana, freed of fearful superstition, not quite folkloric, not quite intransient, waiting in ambush for poetry that yearns to be discovered quietly. A poetry requiring nothing more that aging. A poetry confident of itself, that exchanges the habitual senile laments, the cries of impotence of other excellent poets – even those of the elegant elegies from the past – for the celebration of the experiences of an autumnal life as a formidable new adventure, an experience that does nothing else but certifies the lengthening of a life that knows no better than to keep on living. There is no time to lose.

The whole book burns with an enthusiasm for love that beats calmly when all is clear, when there is no need to think, when life's apparently new inertia drags you down mountainside. Love is what renews life again and again, its greatest, most well-guarded secret, or perhaps the great lie with which the poets trick us. Either way, it is the authentic artificial paradise, the hardest drug ever to be experienced by human beings. At the end of this great book the reader will discover a certain troubadour-esque dawn where two furtive lovers await the rising sun without habitual laments. Crying is for others. At least for a moment, both have managed to stop thinking about their inevitable separation that, riven with prophetic fatalism, will fall like a dead weight. Not mortified by what is to come, they are the greatest of all lovers in this world because they take advantage of the little time they have to tug a little more on the eternal thread, the pleasure of the senses, the exultant present. When one doesn't have, or doesn't want to have, anything other than the present, this is possible. When life is so well lived, there is no time to think of the inevitable.